CRITTERS OF WISCONSIN
POCKET GUIDE

Produced in cooperation with Wildlife Forever

by Ann E. McCarthy, Director of Education

Adventure Publications, Inc.
Cambridge, Minnesota

Dedication

To the Vezina family of River Falls with appreciation and to Micha[e]l T. Clifford and Mark Hansen in memory of Michael "Fester" Mart[i] of Lake Geneva. Best wishes to my former students, today's con servationists.

– Ann E. McCarth[y]

Special thanks to Mary Kay Salwey and Matt McKay of the Wisconsi[n] Department of Natural Resources.

Technical Reviewers: Mary Kay Salwey and Bill Volkert, WI DNR

Project Coordinator: Brett Richardson

Cover, interior design and illustrations: Jonathan Norberg

Photo Credits: **Dominique Braud:** 76 (perching) **Dominique Braud/DPA:** 102 **Mary Clay/DPA:** 80 **Sharon Cummings/DPA:** 20, 96 (male), 104 **E.[R]. Degginger/DPA:** 44 **Dan Dempster/DPA:** 88 (female) **Dudley Edmondson:** 24, 30, 34 (winter), 76 (soaring), 84 (soaring), 110 (male) **Joh[n] Gerlach/DPA:** 46 **Richard Haug:** 38 **Randall B. Henne/DPA:** 52 **Ada[m] Jones/DPA:** 64, 66 (female), 88 (male), 90 (display) **Rolf Kopfle/DPA:** 9[?] **Greg W. Lasley/KAC Productions:** 72 **Bill Lea/DPA:** 16 **Doug Locke/DPA:** 58, 96 (female) **Bill Marchel:** 32, 62 (female) **Gary Meszaros/DPA:** 4[?] **John Mielcarek/DPA:** 26 **Skip Moody/DPA:** 14, 28 (male), 66 (male), 8[?] (perching) **Alan Nelson/DPA:** 12, 18, 48 **Stan Osolinski/DPA:** 56 (sum mer) **Rod Planck/DPA:** 98 **Maslowski Productions:** 22, 34 (summer) 36, 42, 56 (winter), 60, 94, 108, 110 (female) **Carl R. Sams II/DPA:** 7[4] 78, 106 **George Stewart/DPA:** 100 **Stan Tekiela:** 28 (female), 50, 54, 6[?] (male), 68, 70, 82, 86, 90 (main)
DPA=Dembinsky Photo Associates

Published by Adventure Publications, Inc.
820 Cleveland Street South
Cambridge, MN 55008
1-800-678-7006
www.adventurepublications.net
All rights reserved
Printed in China
ISBN-10: 1-59193-134-7
ISBN-13: 978-1-59193-134-8

ABOUT WILDLIFE FOREVER

Wildlife Forever is a nonprofit conservation organization dedicated to conserving America's wildlife heritage through education, preservation of habitat and management of fish and wildlife. Working at the grassroots level, Wildlife Forever has completed conservation projects in all 50 states. Wildlife Forever's innovative outreach programs include the Wildlife Forever State-Fish Art Project and the Theodore Roosevelt Conservation Partnership.

Cry of the Wild

The "cry of the wild" can still be heard across this great land. I have heard the bugle of an elk amid the foothills of the western plains…the shrill of a bald eagle along the banks of the mighty Mississippi…the roar of a brown bear on windswept tundra…the thunder of migrating waterfowl on coastal shores…the gobble of a wild turkey among eastern hardwoods and the haunting cry of a sandhill crane in the wetlands of the Central Flyway. America is truly blessed—a land rich in natural resources. This legacy must be preserved.

I hope this book will provide you with an insight to the many wonders of the natural world and serve as a stepping-stone to the great outdoors.

Yours for wildlife…forever,

Douglas H. Grann
President & CEO, Wildlife Forever

To learn more contact us at 763-253-0222, 2700 Freeway Blvd., Ste. 1000, Brooklyn Center, MN 55430 or check out our website at www.wildlifeforever.org.

TABLE OF CONTENTS

FOREWORD
by Secretary Scott Hassett

Wisconsin's wild areas are great places to explore. Our wi
birds and mammals make your experience very mem
rable.

Each season offers unique wildlife viewing opportunities.
spring, watch the return of thousands of migratory bird
from Red-winged Backbirds to Canada Geese. In summe
keep a sharp eye out for river otters playing along the bank
of the Mississippi River or Chippewa Flowage. A visit to cer
tral Wisconsin in fall provides awesome sights and sound
of migrating Sandhill Cranes. In our great northwoods liste
for the howls of gray wolves in winter or to the bugling of e
in October. In our cold months, take a moment to check th
open waters near dams along the Wisconsin River f
majestic Bald Eagles as they fish the icy waters. At night, lis
ten to the howls of coyotes or the hoots of Barred Owls.

Regardless of where you live, wildlife is all around you. A
you need to do is take the time to look. Enjoy!

P. Scott Hassett

Scott Hassett
Secretary
Wisconsin Department of Natural Resources
101 South Webster Street
Madison, WI 53707
www.dnr.state.wi.us/

WISCONSIN'S WILD PLACES

Wisconsin has over 1.5 million acres of public land where you and your family can watch wildlife and pursue a variety of other activities such as hiking, nature study, snowshoeing, canoeing, hunting or fishing.

State Wildlife Areas generally have only minor facility development such as small unpaved parking lots and no groomed trails. You can wander at will on these lands, except in areas posted as Wildlife Refuges.

State Parks have a greater number of amenities such as hiking and interpretive trails, campgrounds, picnic areas, restrooms and concessions.

- State Forests also provide hiking, camping and areas open to hunting and fishing. For more information about where to watch wildlife, explore www.dnr.state.wi.us.

FACTS
About Wisconsin

Wisconsin. The name means gathering of the waters or place of the beaver and comes from the Algonquian Indian word Ouisconsin.

Glaciers (massive sheets of ice) formed Wisconsin's four major geographical regions over a million years ago. The Northern Highland region, also called the North Woods, is made up of dense forests and expansive wetlands. The Central Plain region lies south of the Northern Highland region. It is largely made up of wetlands and prairie grasslands. The Eastern Ridges and Lowlands region is made up of gentle, rolling hills. Its fertile soil makes it well-suited for agriculture. The Western Upland (Driftless) region was untouched by glacier flow. It is made up of scenic river valleys and sandstone bluffs.

Shaped like a mitten, Wisconsin is almost entirely surrounded by water with the Mississippi River to the west, Lake Michigan to the east and Lake Superior to the north. (Lake Superior is the largest freshwater lake in the world.) Wisconsin ranks third in the country for overall water with some fifteen thousand lakes and several major rivers including the Fox, Saint Croix, Wisconsin, Rock and Wolf.

Wisconsin's natural beauty is dramatic and varied. Treasured national forests, lakeshores and refuges, including Nicolet National Forest, Apostle Islands National Lakeshore and Necedah National Wildlife Refuge, contain amazing beauty in their rugged cliffs, deep gorges, ancient forests, sandy beaches, rich wetlands and colorful prairies.

ountless species of wildlife, including black bear, coyote, white-tailed deer, Common Loon, Bald Eagle, Ringed-necked Pheasant, Red-tailed Hawk and Great Blue Heron, find vital, healthy habitat in Wisconsin. During spring and fall, about 00,000 birds use Horicon National Wildlife Refuge as a stopover during their migration.

Wisconsin has a long tradition of conservation, and is home to many famous conservationists including Aldo Leopold (father of Wildlife Management), John Muir (founder of the Sierra Club) and Gaylord Nelson (founder of Earth Day).

Wisconsin abounds with recreation opportunities, with 56 state parks and 20 state trails including Aztalan State Park, Big Bay State Park, Governor Dodge State Park, White River State Trail and Kettle Moraine State Forest. These places are ideal for skiing, hunting, fishing, snowshoeing, hiking, birding and canoeing. Wisconsin is a great place for wildlife and for people who enjoy the great outdoors.

State Bird:	State Flower:	State Fish:
American Robin	Wood Violet	Muskellunge
State Animal:	**State Wildlife Animal:**	**State Tree:**
American Badger	White-tailed Deer	Sugar Maple
State Mineral:	**State Rock:**	**State Insect:**
Galena	Red Granite	Honeybee
State Motto:	**State Nickname:**	**State Symbol of Peace:**
Forward	Badger State or America's Dairyland	Mourning Dove

Wisconsin is nicknamed the Badger State because lead miners in the 1800s tunneled deep into the hillsides—much like badgers.

HOW TO USE THIS GUIDE

While this book is not intended as a field guide (we don'
want anyone getting too close to a bear trying to identify it
species!), it is intended to be a great reference for informa
tion on some of the fascinating animals that we loosely ca
the "critters" of Wisconsin. We think that the more informa
tion people have about wildlife and their needs, the more w
can do to conserve this wonderful part of our natural world

Notes About Icons

In the mammal section, the track c
one foot is included near the bottor
right of the page. The size, from top t
bottom is included. When appropriate
the front and hind print are include
with the front placed at the top of th
oval, and the hind at the bottom. Note that for som
animals, the hind print actually appears ahead of the fron
This will be apparent in the layout of the tracks as shown i
the right margin. While the sizes of the individual tracks ar
relative to each other, the pattern of tracks is not. We woul
have needed a very large page to accommodate the el
tracks compared to the chipmunk!

The animal/person silhouette on the bo
tom left of the mammal pages is to sho
the relative size of the animal compare
to an average-sized adult. Sometime
it's easier to judge comparisons tha
actual measurements.

nocturnal (active at night)

diurnal (active during day)

crepuscular (most active at dawn and dusk)

Zzz *hibernator/deep sleeper* (dormant during winter)

The yellow symbols depicting the sun, moon or the sun on the horizon indicate whether the animal is nocturnal, diurnal or crepuscular. While you may see these animals at other times, they are most active during the periods shown. The yellow Zzzs indicate whether or not the animal hibernates. Some critters are true hibernators, which means their body processes slow down a great deal and they require very little energy to survive the winter. Other critters are deep sleepers, and their body processes slow down only a little and they require greater amounts of energy to survive the winter.

| cup | ground | platform | cavity |

On the bird pages, the nest type is shown at the bottom right. This indicates whether the bird builds a cup-type nest, a ground nest, a platform nest or a cavity nest.

On the Lifelist on page 112, place a check by each mammal or bird you've seen, whether in your backyard or at the zoo.

DID YOU KNOW...? The American Badger is the state animal of Wisconsin. It uses its digging ability to dig itself out of trouble. It can dig at a faster rate than a person can dig with a shovel. While digging, the badger sends dirt flying 4–5' into the air. Although the badger has very short legs and walks in a pigeon-toed fashion (toes pointed in), it can still reach speeds of 10–15 mph.

BADGER, AMERICAN

Taxidea taxus

Size: body 20–35" long; tail 4–6" long: stands 9" high at shoulder; weighs 13–30 lbs.

Habitat: dry, open grasslands, prairies and farmlands

Range: throughout Wisconsin

Food: snakes, chipmunks, woodchucks, rabbits, thirteen-lined ground squirrel, turtle eggs, ground-nesting birds' eggs; may burrow into dens of some of these prey

Den: grass-lined; located 2–6' underground

Young: 3–7 young born blind between March and April after a gestation of about 7 months; eyes open at 4–6 weeks; nurse for 4–6 weeks; later learn to hunt; independent at 10–12 weeks

Predators: few; coyotes, bobcats and domestic dogs

Tracks: show 5 toes and a soft, medium-sized pad, with long claw imprints

Description: The American Badger has a wide, flattened body with short fur that is silver-gray to yellowish gray. It has a broad, wedge-shaped head with a white stripe that runs from the nose, over the head and down the back. It has short, powerful legs with 2" claws and spends most of the time underground.

2¼"

mammals

DID YOU KNOW...? The bat is the only mammal capable of flight. It uses echolocation (sound waves) to detect and catch insects. It is capable of catching 600 moths in one hour and thousands of mosquitoes in a single night. Each fall, as temperatures begin to drop and the numbers of insects decline, it migrates to favorite hibernation sites. It returns to breeding sites in late spring.

nocturnal   crepuscular   Zzz hibernator

BAT, LITTLE BROWN
Myotis lucifugus

Size: body 3–4½" long with a 1½" forearm; 8–9" wingspan; weighs ¼–⅓ oz.

Habitat: wooded areas near water and large insect populations

Range: throughout Wisconsin

Food: insects including moths, mosquitoes, beetles and crickets

Nest Site: colonize and roost in groups in attics and other buildings, tree cavities and caves

Young: one dark brown pup is born after a gestation of 60 days, commonly in maternity colonies of a few dozen to thousands of females; it weighs 30% of adult and nurses for approximately 4 weeks; able to fly at 3 weeks

Predators: owls, snakes, raccoons, domestic cats

Tracks: none

Description: The Little Brown Bat has a coat of silky cinnamon-buff to dark brown hair, with pale gray undersides and hand-like wings. It skims the water's surface where it catches insects at a rate of one every eight seconds.

no tracks

DID YOU KNOW...? The Black Bear is an excellent climber. It can run at speeds of 25 mph. It loves bee larvae and honey and will rip open a beehive to obtain them. Its thick coat protects it from bee stings. During winter, the Black Bear spends up to three months in its den, living off its stored body fat. Torn-apart logs and destroyed hornet nests may be signs of where bears have been. Black Bears can sometimes be spotted near suburban areas in central and western Wisconsin.

crepuscular   **Zzz** *deep sleeper*

BEAR, BLACK
Ursus americanus

Size: body 4½–6' long; stands 3–3½' high at shoulder; females weigh 100–500 lbs.; males weigh 100–900 lbs.

Habitat: forests, swamps and prairies

Range: central and northern Wisconsin

Food: nuts, roots, berries, insects, fish, mice and other small mammals; will raid trash cans

Den: located in brush piles, hollow logs, under fallen trees or beneath uprooted trees

Young: cubs, usually twins, born between mid-January and mid-February after a gestation of about 60 days; born blind and hairless with pinkish skin; 8" long; weigh 8 oz. each; eyes open at 40 days; cubs nurse and remain in den until spring; independent at 18 months

Predators: adult male black bears may prey on cubs

Tracks: note big toe on outside of foot

Description: The Black Bear's fur is usually black, but it can be light brown or reddish brown. It has a small, narrow head with thick, rounded ears and a brown muzzle.

4"

7–9"

DID YOU KNOW...? A beaver can chew down hundreds of trees each year. One family of beavers may consume as much as a ton (2,000 lbs.) of bark in a single winter. To maintain water level, beavers may build dams up to 100 yards long. It's able to hold its breath for 15 minutes. Look for tree cuttings near the shoreline and mud mounds marked with scent. Listen for tail slaps on the water.

nocturnal   *crepuscular*

BEAVER, AMERICAN
Castor canadensis

Size: body 27–35" long; tail 15" long, 7" wide; weighs 28–75 lbs.

Habitat: freshwater streams, rivers, ponds or lakes bordered by trees

Range: throughout Wisconsin

Food: in spring and summer, leaves, buds, twigs, fruit, ferns, stems and roots of aquatic plants; in fall and winter, bark from tree cuttings stored underwater

Den: lodge; dome-shaped structure, 2–10' tall, 12–14' wide, with underwater entrance

Young: 3–5 kits born with thick dark fur between mid-February and June after a gestation of 100–110 days; weigh 1 lb. each; able to swim soon after birth; nurse for 8–10 weeks; fully independent at 2 years

Predators: coyotes, bobcats and wolves

Tracks: often erased by tail as it drags behind

Description: The beaver is a large rodent with prominent orange teeth and a large, flat, paddle-shaped tail. The beaver is specially adapted to life underwater with waterproof fur, webbed hind feet, goggle-like eyelids and valves that keep water out of its nose and ears.

6"

DID YOU KNOW...? Found only in North America, and the most common wildcat here, the Bobcat is named for its stubby, bobbed tail. It can leap 7–10' in a single bound. An excellent climber, it uses trees for resting, observation and protection. It can travel 3–7 miles for a hunt and stores uneaten food under vegetation. Signs may include scratch marks on trees and shredded bark nearby.

nocturnal   *crepuscular*

BOBCAT
Lynx rufus

Size: body 26–36" long; tail 4–7" long; stands 20–30" high at shoulder; weighs 15–40 lbs.

Habitat: forested areas with open fields; wooded ravines and open bottomlands

Range: northern region; much of central Wisconsin

Food: rabbits, mice, squirrels, mink, muskrat, skunk, fox, porcupine, birds, bats, snakes, frogs and carrion (remains of dead animals)

Den: located in hollow logs, on rocky ledges and in caves and brush piles

Young: 2–3 kittens born blind in April or May after a gestation of 60–70 days; 10" long; weigh 12 oz. each; eyes open a few days after birth; nurse for 8 weeks; begin to eat meat at 4 weeks; fully independent at 5 months

Predators: young taken by fishers, foxes, great horned owls and adult male bobcats

Tracks: large, cat-like with 4 toes and a larger rear pad

Description: The Bobcat has a yellowish gray coat with reddish brown streaks and a sprinkling of black. The fur on its undersides is a soft beige. It is mostly gray during the winter months.

2"

DID YOU KNOW...? The Eastern Chipmunk is able to run 15 feet per second. It uses its outsized cheek pouches to store and carry food. It leaves a trail of chewed nutshells. Its call is a quick "chip-chip-chip." Frost causes it to head for its den, where it spends a few weeks to several months in a deep sleep. It wakes now and then to eat stored food. In the chipmunk's scientific name, *Tamias* means to store, and *striatus* means striped. The Eastern Chipmunk is frequently seen in suburban areas.

diurnal   Zzz deep sleeper

CHIPMUNK, EASTERN
Tamias striatus

Size: body 5–6" long; tail 3–4" long; weighs 2½–4½ oz.

Habitat: forested areas; brush piles, rock piles and stone walls

Range: throughout Wisconsin

Food: nuts, buds, berries, seeds and insects

Den: part of burrow with several chambers including a pantry, bathroom and bedroom; entrance is 1½" across; often found under rock piles, brush piles and tangled roots

Young: 2 litters per year; 1–8 young born blind and hairless between March and May and between July and August after a gestation of 31 days; weigh 0.1 oz. each; fuzzy coat appears at 2 weeks; eyes open at 4 weeks; fully independent at 8 weeks

Predators: weasels, domestic cats, owls, hawks and snakes

Tracks: difficult to find because of small size; front feet show 4 toes, hind feet show 5

Description: The Eastern Chipmunk is reddish brown with five dark stripes alternating with gray; lighter underside.

⅝"

1"

mammals

DID YOU KNOW...? Burrows provide winter cover for the Eastern Cottontail. A group of burrows is called a warren. The cottontail has great eyesight and speed, as well as protective coloring. It is a very important prey species in North America, having many predators. The Eastern Cottontail is frequently seen in suburban areas.

 nocturnal *crepuscular*

COTTONTAIL, EASTERN
Sylvilagus floridanus

Size: body 14–18" long; tail 2" long; weighs 2–4 lbs.

Habitat: woodlands and brushy areas near fields, hedges and fence rows

Range: throughout Wisconsin

Food: in summer, alfalfa, dandelion, clover, berries, garden crops; in winter, tree bark, twigs, shrubs; eats own scat for added food value

Nest Site: 5" deep depression (burrow) lined with plant material and fur; usually found in meadows or at the base of trees

Young: 3–4 litters per year; 4–7 young born hairless and blind between February and October after a gestation of 28 days; 4" long; weigh 1 oz. each; eyes open at 1 week; nurse for 4 weeks; fully independent at 5 weeks

Predators: most carnivores, including foxes, coyotes, bobcats, minks, hawks, owls and bald eagles

Tracks: toe pads don't show clearly, because of thick fur covering the feet

Description: The Eastern Cottontail is a grayish brown rabbit with rusty-colored fur behind its ears. It has a fluffy, cottony white tail.

1"

3½"

mammals

DID YOU KNOW...? Known as the trickster in certain Native American folklore because of its clever ways, the Coyote is unique to North America. It's capable of running at speeds of more than 30 mph. Its distinct howl, coupled with short high-pitched yelps can be heard as far away as 3 miles. The Coyote can sometimes be seen in suburban areas.

 nocturnal   crepuscular   diurnal

COYOTE
Canis latrans

Size: body 32–40" long; tail 12–15" long; stands 15–20" high at shoulder; weighs 18–30 lbs.

Habitat: woodlands, grasslands, prairies and pastures

Range: throughout Wisconsin

Food: small mammals (e.g., mice, squirrels and rabbits), birds, frogs, snakes, fish, carrion (remains of dead animals) on rare occasions and an occasional deer; stores uneaten food under leaves and soil

Den: found in roots of old trees, on hillsides, in gravel pits, in wooded thickets, under hollow logs, or in a bank along the water's edge

Young: 5–10 pups born blind and grayish between March and June after a gestation of 58–63 days; weigh 8 oz. each; eyes open at 8–14 days; pups nurse for several weeks; later both adults feed pups regurgitated food; independent at 6–9 months

Predators: wolves may prey on pups

Tracks: look like medium-sized dog tracks with 4 toes and a rear pad

Description: The Coyote has a light brown to gray coat with reddish sides and pale undersides. It has longer black-tipped fur on its shoulders and a bushy, black-tipped tail.

2½"

female

DID YOU KNOW...? When alarmed, the White-tailed Deer raises its tail, which resembles a white flag. It can run up to 35–40 mph. During the breeding season, males make marks (rubs) on sapling trees with their antlers to make other males aware of their presence. Males spar with each other over females and make scrapes, which are patches of muddy ground where they urinate to attract females. White-tailed Deer can be spotted in suburban areas.

crepuscular

DEER, WHITE-TAILED
Odocoileus virginianus

Size: body 4–6' long; tail 6–13" long; stands 2–3' high at shoulder; males weigh 100–300 lbs., females weigh 85–130 lbs.

Habitat: woodlands, swamplands and grasslands

Range: throughout Wisconsin

Food: in summer, mushrooms, wildflowers and crops; in winter, acorns and bark from willow, oak, birch and maple trees

Bedding Site: shallow depressions in hidden, grassy areas; beds down in a different spot each night

Young: 1 or 2 fawns born with white spots for camouflage between May and August after a gestation of 7 months; weigh 8 lbs. each; spots remain for 3–4 months; fawns nurse for several months; independent at 1 year

Predators: wolves and bears; coyotes and domestic dogs may take fawns

Tracks: narrow, heart-shaped with split hoof

Description: The White-tailed Deer has a reddish brown coat in summer, and a grayish brown coat in winter. Its belly and undertail are white. Each spring, males grow forward-facing antlers that are shed in winter.

mammals

3"

DID YOU KNOW...? Before European settlers arrived in North America, there were approximately 10 million Elk. By the early 1900s, however, the Elk population had dropped significantly. Today, thanks to conservation efforts, the Elk population has grown. The Elk became extinct in Wisconsin at the turn of the century due to unregulated hunting. In 1995, a small herd of 25 animals was reintroduced to northern Wisconsin in the Chequamegon-Nicolet National Forest near Clam Lake. Today the herd count is approximately 120.

crepuscular

ELK

Cervus elaphus

Size: body 5–8' long; tail 3–8" long; stands 2–5' at shoulder; weighs 500–1,000 lbs.

Habitat: open woodlands

Range: reintroduced to northern Wisconsin in Chequamegon-Nicolet National Forest near Clam Lake

Food: grass, buds, herbs and mushrooms in summer; twigs, bark and grass beneath snow in winter

Bedding Site: hidden, grassy or forested areas; beds down in a different spot each night

Young: one calf born tan and speckled with white spots between May and June after a gestation of 8 months; weighs 35 lbs; able to stand shortly after birth; joins herd at 16 days, but nurses for 9 months; develops adult color at 90 days; females form nursery groups to care for calves

Predators: wolves; young taken by bears

Tracks: heart-shaped, similar to white-tailed deer

Description: The Elk is dark brown to reddish brown with a yellowish rump patch. Its legs, neck and belly are darker than the rest of the body. Males (called bulls) grow antlers that measure up to 5' across.

4½"

mammals

DID YOU KNOW...? The Red Fox can leap 15' in a single bound. The fox can run up to 30 mph and is an excellent swimmer. It stores uneaten food under snow or brush piles, especially in winter. The Red Fox can sometimes be spotted in suburban areas. There are four species of fox found in North America: red fox, gray fox, arctic fox and swift fox (the kit fox is a subspecies of the swift fox). Both the Red Fox and the gray fox are found in Wisconsin.

nocturnal   *crepuscular*

FOX, RED
Vulpes vulpes

Size: body 20–40" long; tail 14–16" long; stands 14–16" high at shoulder; weighs 8–15 lbs.

Habitat: open grasslands, marshes and woodlands

Range: throughout Wisconsin

Food: insects, nuts, corn, birds, mice, rabbits and carrion (remains of dead animals)

Den: often found in hilly areas, in tree roots, under woodpiles and in abandoned woodchuck burrows; entrance is 8–15" across

Young: 5–10 kits born charcoal gray between February and May after a gestation of 52 days; weigh 3–8 oz. each; nurse for 10 weeks; later both adults feed them regurgitated food; independent at 7 months

Predators: coyotes and bobcats with rare success

Tracks: small dog-like tracks follow a straight line; claws show

Description: The Red Fox shows several color variations from rusty red to black, silver and dark brown, all with white undersides. It has black legs and a white-tipped tail.

2¼"

summer

winter

DID YOU KNOW...? Named for its very large feet, the Snowshoe Hare is well-suited for travel on snow. It grows extra fur on its hind feet in winter to help keep it from sinking in soft or deep snow. It is very fast, able to reach speeds of up to 30 mph, and it can leap up to 12' in a single bound. Snowshoe Hares are the most important food source for the Canada lynx.

Signs of the hare include yellow to pink urine on snow.

crepuscular

HARE, SNOWSHOE
Lepus americanus

Size: body 17–20" long; tail 2" long; weighs 2–4¼ lbs.

Habitat: dense cover of thickets, evergreen forests, wooded areas and marshes

Range: central and northern Wisconsin

Food: in spring and summer, grass, clover, dandelion, ferns; in fall and winter, bark and twigs of birch, willow, aspen trees, evergreen needles; eats own scat for added nutritional value

Nest Site: depressions on the ground (forms) measuring 4–6" wide and 6–8" long

Young: 2–3 litters per year; 2–4 young born between mid-March and mid-August after a gestation of 36 days; young are fully mobile, covered with fur, and able to see; weigh 2 oz. each; nurse for 4 weeks at which time they are fully independent

Predators: lynx, coyotes, wolves, bobcats, foxes, martens and minks

Tracks: triangular shape; rear tracks resemble snowshoes

Description: The Snowshoe Hare has large hind feet. Its coat is brown in summer and white in winter.

mammals

4–5"

DID YOU KNOW...? In spite of its small size, the Mink is an aggressive predator. It commonly kills prey in their burrows. The Mink may dig its own den, but it often takes over abandoned muskrat burrows and beaver lodges. It seldom stays in its den for long periods, as the mink moves frequently.

nocturnal

MINK
Mustela vison

Size: body 11–20" long; tail 5–9" long; weighs ½–3½ lbs.

Habitat: rivers, lakes, streams, swamps and marshes

Range: throughout Wisconsin

Food: fish, frogs, mice, ducks, eggs, insects, snakes, crayfish, chipmunks, rabbits, muskrats and carrion (remains of dead animals)

Den: lined with fur and grass; usually near waterways, often under tree roots or in abandoned burrows of muskrat or beaver

Young: 2–10 kits born blind and covered with fine white fur between mid-February and May after a gestation of 28–32 days; 1–2" long; weigh 1 oz. each; eyes open at 25 days; nurse for 5 weeks; fully independent at 8 weeks

Predators: owls and coyotes

Tracks: show 4 or 5 toes; often seen along water's edge

Description: The Mink has glossy, rich brown or black fur, with a white chin patch and occasional white spots on the belly. It has small rounded ears and a bushy tail.

mammals

1¾"

DID YOU KNOW...? The Muskrat creates a V-shaped wave as it swims. It can hold its breath for up to 15 minutes. This skill is important as the Muskrat works with cattails, grass and mud to build lodges in the water. The lodges measure up to 6' high and 8' across and a good lodge can be used by several generations for 20 or 30 years. In winter, muskrats gnaw a hole in the ice and push vegetation up through it. These are called pushups and are used as feeding sites.

crepuscular

MUSKRAT
Ondatra zibethicus

Size: body 9–13" long; tail 7–12" long; weighs 2–4 lbs.

Habitat: marshes, ponds, rivers, streams and lakes that have thick vegetation and do not entirely freeze

Range: throughout Wisconsin

Food: water lilies, cattails, fish, frogs, crayfish, snails, apples, carrots, soybeans and clover

Den: underground along the water's edge, or lodges built on platforms

Young: 2–3 litters per year; 1–11 young born blind between March and October after a gestation of 25–30 days; weigh ¾ oz. each; eyes open at 14–18 days; nurse for 3–4 weeks; independent at 4 weeks

Predators: minks, foxes, coyotes, hawks and owls

Tracks: although they have 5 toes on each foot, only 4 show clear imprint; hind feet partly webbed

Description: The Muskrat is a dark reddish brown to black rodent with slightly lighter undersides and a long, rat-like, nearly hairless tail.

1¼"

2"

mammals

DID YOU KNOW...? When cornered, an opossum will fall into a death-like state (therefore the term "playing possum") for up to three hours. It is the only marsupial (pouched) animal native to North America, and it has 50 teeth, more than any other land mammal on this continent. The opossum is an agile climber and good swimmer. It has a prehensile (grasping) tail that it can use to stabilize itself as it walks along tree branches. In winter, and especially during severe weather, it rests in abandoned burrows and hollow trees.

nocturnal   *crepuscular*

OPOSSUM, VIRGINIA
Didelphis virginiana

Size: body 13–20" long; tail 9–15" long; weighs 4–15 lbs.

Habitat: woodlands and brushy areas, commonly near water

Range: westernmost edge and southern and central Wisconsin

Food: worms, reptiles, insects, eggs, grain and carrion (remains of dead animals); will also eat garbage when available

Nest Site: none; immediately after birth, young crawl into mother's kangaroo-like pouch and each attaches to one of 13 nipples

Young: 2 litters per year; 6–20 kits born blind and hairless without well-developed rear limbs between mid-January and May after a gestation of 2 weeks; ½" long; weigh less than 1 oz. each; nurse inside the pouch for 8 weeks, then ride on the mother's back for 4 weeks; fully independent at 12 weeks

Predators: bobcats, coyotes, foxes, domestic dogs, hawks and owls

Tracks: hand-like tracks show "thumb" on hind foot; tail drags between feet

Description: The opossum's body is usually grayish white, but can be nearly black. It has hairless ears and tail, and a white face with a long, pink-nosed snout.

1¾"

mammals

DID YOU KNOW...? The otter's torpedo-shaped body allows it to glide effortlessly through the water. It can tread water and swim on its front, back and sides. It is able to dive to depths of 50' and hold its breath for 6–8 minutes at a time. The otter uses slides or shoreline chutes to enter the water, and it makes otter rolls, which are bowl-shaped areas 20–100' from the water where it dries off and marks territory.

crepuscular

OTTER, NORTHERN RIVER
Lontra canadensis

Size: body 18–32" long; tail 11–20" long; weighs 10–30 lbs.

Habitat: lakes, rivers and streams

Range: throughout Wisconsin

Food: carp, sunfish, perch, trout, bass, minnows, frogs, mussels, snakes, crayfish and turtles

Den: located near water and lined with plant material; may use upturned logs, upturned stumps, muskrat or beaver lodges

Young: 1–5 pups born blind and fur covered between November and March after a gestation of 60–63 days; weigh 5 oz. each; eyes open at 1 month; explore outside the den at 2 months; continue to nurse for 4 months; fully independent at 6 months

Predators: wolves and coyotes

Tracks: often hidden by dragging tail; front and hind feet show 5 toes

Description: The otter is long and sleek with a muscular tail and a dark brown coat. Well-adapted to life in and under the water, it has a layer of insulating fat, dense fur, webbed feet and valves that keep water out of its ears and nose.

3"

DID YOU KNOW...? Approximately 30,000 quills provide the porcupine with a unique defense. When confronted by a would-be attacker, it swats the animal (or person) with its tail, which is loaded with needle-sharp 4" quills. It does not shoot its quills. Barbed ends cause the quills to work their way deeper into the attacker's muscles, making them difficult to extract. It spends the day resting in trees.

PORCUPINE, NORTH AMERICAN
Erethizon dorsatum

Size: body 18–23" long; tail 6–12" long; 10–28 lbs.

Habitat: forested areas, especially northern hardwoods

Range: northern and central Wisconsin

Food: clover, grass, seeds, corn, leaves and evergreen needles, aquatic plants, acorns, bark and twigs

Den: located in hollow logs, tree cavities, under stumps and buildings, in caves and in the abandoned burrows of other animals

Young: a single pup born with dark fur and soft 1" quills between May and July after a gestation of 200–217 days; weighs 1 lb.; pup nurses for 3 months; fully independent at 5 months

Predators: fishers and bobcats

Tracks: show long nails and bumpy pads; often hidden by dragging tail

Description: The porcupine is a large, round-bodied rodent. It has color variations that include blonde, dark gray, dark brown and black. Its quills are actually modified hairs.

2⅝"

3⅜"

mammals

DID YOU KNOW...? The raccoon is an excellent climber and swimmer. Contrary to popular belief, it does not wash everything it eats. Clever and agile, the raccoon is highly adapted to gathering and eating a great variety of foods, and even raids garbage cans. In the fall, it develops a thick layer of fat. It often spends daytime sunbathing in trees.

RACCOON, NORTHERN
Procyon lotor

Size: body 16–28" long; tail 8–12" long; stands 12" high at the shoulder; weighs 15–40 lbs.

Habitat: wooded areas near fields, rivers and ponds

Range: throughout Wisconsin

Food: nuts, berries, insects, fish, crayfish, frogs, bird and turtle eggs, garden vegetables, grain, rodents and carrion (remains of dead animals); will raid trash cans

Den: found in hollow trees, woodchuck burrows, culverts and under buildings

Young: 2–7 young born in February or March after a gestation of 63 days; born blind, with a light fur covering, a faint mask, and ringed tail; 4" long; weigh 2 oz. each; eyes open at 21 days; nurse for several weeks; leave den at 10 weeks; fully independent at 4–6 months

Predators: coyotes, foxes, bobcats and great horned owls

Tracks: small, hand-like prints

Description: The raccoon has heavy fur streaked brown, black and gray with a distinctive black face mask and a bushy, ringed tail.

3"

DID YOU KNOW...? The skunk is famous for defending itself with a foul-smelling spray it squirts up to 15'. Even a 3-week-old kit can spray! Before spraying, a skunk usually hisses, stomps its front feet and waves its tail in warning. Although skunks are blamed for those smells along woods, fields and trails, fox and coyote mark their territories with a strong musky scent very similar to that of a skunk. The Striped Skunk can sometimes be spotted in suburban areas.

nocturnal   Zzz *deep sleeper*

SKUNK, STRIPED
Mephitis mephitis

Size: body 15" long; tail 7–8"; weighs 3–10 lbs.

Habitat: woodlands, pastures and bottomlands with thick vegetation; usually near water

Range: throughout Wisconsin

Food: mice, voles, chipmunks, insects, berries, fruit and bird and turtle eggs; will also eat garbage when available

Den: grass and leaf-lined dens under wood piles, in culverts and under buildings

Young: 5–7 kits born blind in April and May after a gestation of 62–66 days; black and white pattern is already apparent in their thin hair; weigh 7 oz. each; eyes open at 3 weeks; weaned at 8 weeks; independent at 10 weeks

Predators: few; domestic dogs, great horned owls and bobcats have been known to attack

Tracks: show five toes across each foot

Description: The Striped Skunk has a glossy black coat with a thin white stripe between the eyes and a broad white -shaped stripe on its back and down its bushy tail.

mammals

1"

DID YOU KNOW...? The Eastern Fox Squirrel is the largest species of tree squirrel. It uses its curved claws for climbing and its tail for balance. It is a member of the Rodentia (rodent) order, which represents over 40% of all mammals and includes such animals as squirrels, mice, chipmunks and beavers. Like all rodents, the fox squirrel has chisel-like, self-sharpening teeth that grow continuously. The fox squirrel is slightly larger than the gray squirrel.

diurnal   crepuscular

SQUIRREL, EASTERN FOX
Sciurus niger

Size: body 10–15" long; tail 9–14" long; weighs 1½–3 lbs.

Habitat: open woodlands of nut producing trees, often near water

Range: throughout Wisconsin, except extreme north

Food: acorns, hickory nuts, walnuts, tree buds, bird eggs, berries, insects, corn and fruit; caches food

Nest Site: a winter or spring litter is born in a tree hollow; a summer litter is born in a 15" ball-shaped treetop nest (drey) made of leaves and twigs approximately 25' above ground; nests are lined with moss, fur, feathers or lichen

Young: 2 litters per year; 2–4 young born blind and hairless between mid-February and April or mid-June to August after a gestation of 6–7 weeks; weigh ½ oz.; eyes open in 5 weeks; nurse for 8 weeks; leave nest at 10 weeks; fully independent at 12 weeks

Predators: red-tailed hawks, great horned owls, barred owls, bald eagles, coyotes and bobcats

Tracks: front print is fairly rounded, hind foot shows five toes and is about 2½" long

Description: The fox squirrel has three distinct color phases: in the north and east it is gray with yellowish undersides, in the west it is reddish and in the south it is almost black.

2½"

mammals

DID YOU KNOW...? Commonly called a gopher, the Thirteen-lined Ground Squirrel is a rodent that hibernates for up to 6 months without food or water. It fattens itself up during the spring and summer, and during the winter its metabolic rate drops and body temperature lowers to only a few degrees above freezing. This is called the torpor state and it allows for a very slow burning of the stored body fat. It will sometimes make tunnels in lawns and golf courses.

○ *diurnal*   **Zzz** *hibernator*

SQUIRREL, THIRTEEN-LINED GROUND

Spermophilus tridecemlineatus

Size: body 6–7" long; tail 3–4" long; weighs 5–7½ oz.

Habitat: short-grass prairies, meadows and pastures

Range: throughout Wisconsin, except extreme north

Food: grasses, roots, insects and seeds; occasionally mice and carrion (remains of dead animals)

Nest Site: burrows about 23' long with 2" openings

Young: 2–13 young born blind in April to May after a gestation of about 28 days, young are hairless and toothless; ⅛ ounce at birth; nurse for 4 weeks; independent at 6 weeks

Predators: foxes, coyotes, badgers and hawks

Tracks: hind foot track shows the long claws that help with digging

Description: The Thirteen-lined Ground Squirrel has 13 alternating dark and light stripes. The dark stripes are brown or black and have buff-colored spots, and the light stripes are light yellow or cream. It has long claws on its hind feet and short ears.

1¼"

mammals

DID YOU KNOW...? The most widespread vole in North America, the Meadow Vole is the primary food source for owls, hawks and falcons. The average life span is less than one year in the wild. Like most small animals, the Meadow Vole has a very high birth rate and a very high death rate. The female reaches sexual maturity at 25 days and is capable of breeding almost immediately after giving birth. The male reaches sexual maturity at 45 days. Look for small tunnels or runways in tall grasses and melting snow.

nocturnal   diurnal

VOLE, MEADOW
Microtus pennsylvanicus

Size: body 4–5" long; tail 1½–2½" long; weighs 1–2½ oz.

Habitat: meadows, moist grasslands, open woodlands and marshes

Range: throughout Wisconsin

Food: grasses, nuts, fruits, leaves, roots, bark and stems; stores and caches food

Nest Site: 6" lined chamber with connecting tunnels

Young: 2–3 litters per year; 4–5 young born between March and November after a gestation of 21 days; weaned at 14 days

Predators: coyotes, foxes, weasels, minks, opossums, snakes, hawks, owls and falcons

Tracks: hind prints show 5 toes; front prints show 4; individual tracks are almost impossible to see, but trail of tracks is visible

Description: The Meadow Vole is blackish brown to reddish brown with gray undersides. It has small eyes and short ears. Its tail is half the length of its body. The male and female are similar in appearance. Like all rodents, the Meadow Vole has 2 pair of incisors at the front of its mouth that are continuously growing.

½"
¾"

summer

winter

DID YOU KNOW...? The Long-tailed Weasel must eat two-thirds of its body weight each day. A ferocious predator, it attacks prey up to five times its size and can be a threat to domestic poultry. The tip of its tail remains black to distract its own predators. Three different species of weasels live in Wisconsin: long-tailed weasel, short-tailed weasel and least weasel.

WEASEL, LONG-TAILED
Mustela frenata

Size: body 8–10" long; tail 3–6" long; weighs 7–12 oz.

Habitat: swamps, farmlands and open woodlands

Range: throughout Wisconsin

Food: frogs, waterfowl, rabbits, mice, muskrats, squirrels and chickens; stores uneaten food

Den: lined with fur and grass; found in rock piles, hollow logs or abandoned burrows

Young: 3–9 young born blind and hairless between March and May after a gestation of 25–35 days; weigh ⅒ oz. each; eyes open at 35 days; young nurse for 3½ weeks; fully independent at 3–4 months

Predators: bobcats, foxes, domestic cats, hawks and owls

Tracks: often seen in a cluster due to running and leaping, rather than in a straight line; show 4 heavily furred toes

Description: The Long-tailed Weasel is a long, slender animal that is usually dark brown in summer and white in winter with a black-tipped tail.

mammals

1¾"

DID YOU KNOW...? The Gray Wolf is also known as the timber wolf. It lives and hunts in packs of 6–12 family members. The pack maintains a strong social structure, with one dominant pair, called the alpha pair. Packs occupy a territory of about 100 square miles and will travel 25–30 miles in pursuit of prey. The Gray Wolf is capable of reaching speeds of 25–40 mph. It has keen hearing and sense of smell. Gray Wolves howl as a means of communication.

diurnal

WOLF, GRAY
Canis lupus

Size: body 40–52" long; tail 13–19" long; stands 26–32" high at shoulder; weighs 60–130 lbs.

Habitat: northern forests and prairies

Range: northernmost Wisconsin

Food: white-tailed deer, elk, small mammals (e.g., mice and rabbits), birds, berries and insects; pack members work together to hunt and kill prey

Den: usually dug by pregnant female; located in hillside or rocky outcrop; used for 8–10 weeks and can be reused for many years

Young: 4–6 pups born blind with a dark coat between March and April after a gestation of 63 days; weigh 1 lb. each; eyes open at 2 weeks; pups nurse for 6–8 weeks; fed regurgitated meat and cared for by pack members; pups begin to hunt with the pack at 6 months; fully grown at 1 year; independent at 2–3 years

Predators: no natural predators

Tracks: similar to large dog's; show claw marks, 4 toes and 1 pad

Description: The Gray Wolf is the largest wild dog in North America. It usually has a gray coat, but color variations include black, brown, reddish, cream or even white. It has short, pointed ears and a long, bushy tail.

4⅝"

DID YOU KNOW...? A Woodchuck can dig a tunnel 5' long in one day. Their burrows often contain a network of tunnels up to 40' long. An active burrow usually has fresh dirt in front of it and has many entrances. A Woodchuck spends time sunning near a burrow entrance. It begins hibernating as early as September and remains in the burrow for up to six months.

The Woodchuck is also known as the whistle pig, marmot, and groundhog, but despite having Groundhog's Day named for it, it cannot really predict when winter will end.

crepuscular **Zzz** *hibernator*

WOODCHUCK
Marmota monax

Size: body 12–23" long; tail 4–10" long; weighs 4–14 lbs.

Habitat: brushy areas, pastures and open woodlands

Range: throughout Wisconsin

Food: alfalfa, fruit, clover, daisies, dandelions, shrubs and garden vegetables

Nest Site: grass-lined burrows, located 4½' under ground

Young: 2–6 young born blind and hairless between March and May after a gestation of 28–30 days; 4" long; weigh 1 oz. each; nurse for 4 weeks; fully independent at 3 months

Predators: red foxes, domestic dogs and timber rattlesnakes

Tracks: front print shows 4 toes, hind print shows 5; rarely seen

Description: The Woodchuck is a large ground mammal with coarse yellow-brown to black fur, short legs and ears, a blunt nose and bushy tail.

mammals

3"

female

male

DID YOU KNOW...? Male and female Red-winged Blackbirds do not migrate together. The males return to breeding areas several weeks before the females, as soon as the snow recedes. The male establishes and defends a nesting site to attract one or more females. During migration, they often flock with other species of blackbirds, such as grackles and cowbirds.

BLACKBIRD, RED-WINGED
Agelaius phoeniceus

Size: body 7½–9½" long; 10–13" wingspan; 1.8 oz.

Habitat: wetlands and grasslands

Range: throughout Wisconsin

Food: seeds and insects

Nesting: early spring

Nest: bowl-shaped; attached to marsh reeds about 12" above water; cattails provide protection from weather and predators

Eggs: average clutch 3–4; pale blue marked with purple and black spots and streaks; 2–3 broods per year

Young: hatch blind and featherless in 10–12 days; eyes open at 1 week; flight feathers develop at 10 days; young leave nesting area at 20 days; females tend the eggs; males defend the nest

Predators: sharp-shinned hawks, northern harriers, great horned owls

Migration: migrates to southern states, Mexico and Central America

Description: Male Red-winged Blackbirds are black with bright red and gold wing patches (epaulets). Females are streaked brown-and-white.

birds

DID YOU KNOW...? The beloved Eastern Bluebird has tremendous eyesight. It is capable of seeing an insect 100 feet away. In the fall, it may form large roosting flocks of up to 50 birds that huddle together at night to conserve heat. The bluebird will generally return to the same nesting site year after year if it is properly maintained.

BLUEBIRD, EASTERN
Sialia sialis

Size: body 7" long; 13" wingspan; 1.1 oz.

Habitat: meadows, open wooded areas and orchards

Range: throughout Wisconsin

Food: insects, seeds and berries

Nesting: April to July

Nest: tree cavities such as woodpecker holes and nesting boxes 5–12' above ground; 4–5 day nest construction primarily built by the female; the nest is lined with feathers or fine grasses

Eggs: average clutch of 3–6; pale blue; 2 broods per year

Young: hatch blind and featherless in 13–15 days; eyes open at 1 week; fully feathered within 2 weeks; leave the nest at 3 weeks; male and female care for the young for up to 4 weeks

Predators: small mammals, snakes and other birds including house sparrows, starlings and wrens that kill the young and take over the nest

Migration: migrates to southern states

Description: Male Eastern Bluebirds are bright blue with a rust-colored breast and white undersides. Females are grayish blue with a rust-colored breast and white undersides.

birds

female

male

DID YOU KNOW...? The Northern Cardinal is very territorial. It has been known to attack its reflection in windows. It's named after the red-robed Cardinals of the Roman Catholic Church. Seven states have identified the cardinal as their state bird, more than any other bird. Both male and female Northern Cardinals sing.

CARDINAL, NORTHERN
Cardinalis cardinalis

Size: body 7–9" long; 12" wingspan; about 1½ oz.

Habitat: wooded areas

Range: throughout Wisconsin

Food: insects, seeds, fruit and berries

Nesting: April to August; during courtship males can be seen feeding females, especially at feeders

Nest: often found in pine trees; constructed of twigs and lined with grass

Eggs: average clutch 3–4; pale blue spotted with brown; 3–4 broods per year

Young: hatch blind and featherless in 12–13 days; eyes open at 1 week; flight feathers develop at 10 days; young leave nesting area at 20 days; both parents care for young

Predators: Cooper's hawks, sharp-shinned hawks, great horned owls, domestic cats

Migration: present year-round

Description: Male cardinals are bright red with a prominent crest and a black face. The females are brownish yellow with a hint of red; both have a large, reddish orange, cone-shaped bill.

birds

DID YOU KNOW...? The Black-capped Chickadee is an incredibly acrobatic little bird, hopping along trees as it searches for food. It also has specialized leg muscles that allow it to hang upside-down on a branch while feeding. It can slowly climb up a nearly vertical tree. "Chicka-dee-dee-dee" is the frequently heard call of the Black-capped Chickadee and the origin of its name. Chickadees form flocks in early fall that last until early spring.

CHICKADEE, BLACK-CAPPED
Poecile atricapillus

Size: body 5–5½" long; 8" wingspan; ½ oz.

Habitat: mixed hardwood-coniferous forests

Range: throughout Wisconsin

Food: insects, seeds and berries

Nesting: between April and June

Nest: excavates holes in dead tree; also uses bird houses and existing cavities from other birds such as woodpeckers; fur or feather lined

Eggs: average clutch 4–9; creamy white with red or purple speckles; 1 brood per year

Young: hatch blind and featherless in 12–13 days; eyes open at 1 week; flight feathers appear at 10–14 days; fly at 14–18 days; female tends young although male brings food to female

Predators: American kestrels, northern shrikes, eastern screech-owls, sharp-shinned hawks

Migration: present year-round

Description: The Black-capped Chickadee has a short, plump body, with a black cap and throat, white cheeks and belly, and a gray back and tail. Its sides are tan. Males are slightly larger than females.

birds

DID YOU KNOW...? The Sandhill Crane travels up to 300 miles a day during its migration. In the spring, males and females perform an elaborate courtship display that involves singing, bowing, skipping and leaping as high as 15–20' into the air. In the 1920s, Wisconsin was home to barely 300 cranes. Today, about 12,000 reside here from spring through fall.

CRANE, SANDHILL
Grus canadensis

Size: body 4' long; 6½' wingspan; 6–12 lbs.

Habitat: wetland areas, usually near open fields

Range: throughout Wisconsin

Food: omnivorous ground feeders; insects, small mammals, amphibians, reptiles, bulbs, seeds and waste grain

Nesting: March to May; male and female return to the same nesting site each spring

Nest: constructed out of plant material and located on the ground near water

Eggs: average clutch 2; large, drab olive to buff spotted with brown; 1 brood per year

Young: hatch in 28–32 days covered with down and able to feed themselves; able to fly at 2–3 months; fully independent at about 1 year

Predators: bobcats, coyotes and bald eagles; foxes prey on eggs

Migration: migrates to southeastern states

Description: The Sandhill Crane is gray with a dark red cap on its head and red eyes. Sometimes its plumage appears to be rusty brown because of staining. It has a very long neck, beak and legs.

birds

DID YOU KNOW...? The original range of the Whooping Crane included both coasts and much of the Midwest. Because of wetland drainage and poaching, the Whooper population dropped from close to 2,000 in the late 1800s to 21 or less by 1941. With only about 200 birds in the wild, it is one of the rarest on the continent and remains on the Endangered Species List. The first hand-reared birds were released into the wild in Wisconsin in 2001. Each year, new birds are reared from a captive flock until the population is able to sustain itself.

CRANE, WHOOPING
Grus americana

Size: body 4–5' long; 7–8' wingspan; 9–17 lbs.

Habitat: shallow wetlands (bogs, marshes and wet grasslands) and agricultural lands

Range: reintroduced to Necedah National Wildlife Refuge near Tomah

Food: clams, insects, fish, rodents, snakes, berries, grains, acorns, crabs, crayfish, plants, frogs

Nesting: April to May; elaborate courtship display of leaping, bobbing and flapping; mates for life

Nest: mounded platform in marshy wetlands

Eggs: average clutch 1–3; tan or cream with brown blotches; 1 brood per year

Young: hatch in 29–31 days, covered with down and fully mobile; dependent on adults for food; usually only one chick per clutch survives; leave nest in 50 days; fledge in 80–90 days; attain full adult plumage in about 2 years

Predators: coyotes and eagles; foxes preys on eggs

Migration: aided by ultralight planes, the new population is learning to fly from Wisconsin to Florida

Description: The Whooping Crane is the tallest bird in North America. It is almost all white, except for some black on its wingtips and red on the crown, forehead and behind the bill. Its long, pointed bill is dark yellow and its legs and feet are black. It has good sight.

birds

DID YOU KNOW...? The Wood Duck is commonly called Woodie. Population numbers declined drastically in the early 1900s due to wetland drainage, unregulated hunting and logging. An experimental nesting box project was initiated in an attempt to boost the Wood Duck population. Today, with the assistance of nest boxes, strict hunting regulations and natural forest growth, Wood Duck populations are very strong. Wood Ducks have broad wings that make a distinct flapping sound as they fly.

DUCK, WOOD
Aix sponsa

Size: body 18½" long; 30" wingspan; 1½ lbs.

Habitat: wooded areas near water

Range: throughout Wisconsin

Food: insects, acorns, hickory nuts, seeds of aquatic plants, grains and fruit

Nesting: March to July

Nest: abandoned woodpecker holes, natural cavities or artificial nesting boxes 20–50' above ground; lined with down; adults often return to same nesting site each year

Eggs: average clutch 8–15; white; 1 brood per year; egg-dumping is common (egg dumping means a female lays one or more eggs in another nest where they are cared for)

Young: hatch in 28–31 days; jump from the nest within 24 hours of hatching; can feed themselves immediately; able to fly at 8–9 weeks

Predators: raccoons preys on eggs; fish, hawks, snapping turtles and otters prey on young

Migration: migrates to southern states

Description: Male Wood Ducks have red eyes and a distinct crest on the head. They are brilliantly colored with iridescent shades of chestnut, purple and green. Females are grayish brown, which camouflages them from predators.

birds

soaring

DID YOU KNOW...? Unique to North America, the Bald Eagle was chosen as our nation's symbol in 1782, narrowly beating out the Wild Turkey. A powerful bird of prey, the Bald Eagle catches its prey with its razor-sharp talons by swooping down at speeds of 50 mph. It was placed on the Federal Endangered Species list in 1972 due to agricultural pesticide contamination. Since the pesticide DDT was banned, the Bald Eagle population has fully recovered, and it is no longer considered to be an endangered species.

EAGLE, BALD
Haliaeetus leucocephalus

Size: body 3–3½' long; 6½–8' wingspan; 8–14 lbs.

Habitat: forested areas near rivers and lakes

Range: throughout Wisconsin

Food: fish make up 90% of diet; regurgitates pellets of indigestible parts of prey

Nesting: March to July; mated pairs return to the same nest site each spring

Nest: located in tall trees

Eggs: average clutch 1–3; large, dull-white; 1 brood per year; male and female care for eggs

Young: eaglets hatch covered with gray down in 35 days; 4 oz. each; male and female care for young; by 10–12 weeks grow brown feathers flecked with white; develop adult coloration, including white head, at 4–5 years

Predators: bobcats, foxes, raccoons, ravens, crows, gulls and owls take young and eggs

Migration: some migrate to southeastern states, though many remain near the Mississippi River in west central Wisconsin during winter

Description: The Bald Eagle is a large, dark brown bird with a white head and tail. Its eyes, beak and feet are bright yellow. Large flocks may gather at feeding grounds during spring or fall migrations.

birds

DID YOU KNOW...? The Canada Goose is nicknamed honker because of the distinct honking sound it makes. Not all honkers migrate, but some travel from winter resting and feeding grounds in the south to summer nesting grounds in the north. They migrate in V-shaped flocks, sometimes flying 1,500 miles round-trip. The Canada Goose has more extreme size variations than any other bird because there are as many as 10 subspecies. The Cackling Canada Goose weighs only 3 lbs., while the Giant Canada Goose weighs more than 12 lbs.

GOOSE, CANADA
Branta canadensis

Size: body 22–40" long; 5–6' wingspan; 2–18 lbs.

Habitat: lakes, ponds, marshes and rivers

Range: throughout Wisconsin

Food: aquatic plants, insects, grass seeds, crops

Nesting: April to May; pairs mate for life

Nest: constructed on a raised site near the water's edge

Eggs: average clutch 5; large and creamy white; 1 brood per year

Young: hatch covered with yellowish down in 28–29 days; leave the nest within 12–14 hours; both parents tend young

Predators: larger meat-eating mammals, great horned owls; goslings may be taken by snapping turtles

Migration: some migrate to southern states; many remain year-round near open water in south-eastern Wisconsin and near the Mississippi River

Description: The Canada Goose is a large, light gray goose with a white chinstrap. It has a black head, neck, bill and feet. Its tracks are triangular and webbed.

birds

Did You Know...? The Ruffed Grouse gets its name from the ruff of dark feathers on each side of its neck. Its wings are short and wide for rapid bursts of flight; it can reach speeds of 40 mph. It has special comb-like membranes on its feet, allowing it to walk easily across the snow. On bitter cold days, it may burrow into the snow, which provides insulated shelter like an igloo.

GROUSE, RUFFED

Bonasa umbellus

Size: body 16–19" long; 22–25" wingspan; 1½ lbs.

Habitat: rural, dense woodlands with open areas

Range: throughout Wisconsin, except extreme southeast

Food: in summer, ferns, mushrooms, seeds, berries and frogs; in winter, aspen and willow buds, sumac, thorn apple; young feed on insects

Nesting: April to June; males stand on a log and "drum" the air by flapping their wings vigorously, creating a "thump, thump, thump" sound that can be heard up to a half mile away

Nest: hens build nest on ground, often at base of trees

Eggs: average clutch 9–12; creamy white; 1 brood per year

Young: hatch in 21–24 days covered with feathers and able to feed themselves; young can fly short distances at 12 days; they stay with female for 3–4 months

Predators: foxes, coyotes, great horned owls, northern goshawks and Cooper's hawks

Migration: present year-round

Description: The Ruffed Grouse is a gray chicken-like bird with flecks of black, white and brown. It has a squared, fan-shaped tail and a crown-like tuft of feathers on its head.

birds

DID YOU KNOW...? The very common Ring-billed Gull takes advantage of many kinds of food in many places and can be seen catching fish in ponds or lakes, following ships on the lakes or farm tractors in plowed fields, as well as scavenging at dumps, parking lots and along lake shores. The Ring-billed Gull is a member of the Laridae family whose name is derived from Latin *larus* for seabird. Its long, slender wings allow it to glide for extended periods of time as it makes use of updrafts of air from waves, dunes and cliffs.

GULL, RING-BILLED
Larus delawarensis

Size: body 18–20" long; 48" wingspan; 1 lb.

Habitat: wetlands, islands in open water and shores of lakes, and in agricultural fields

Range: throughout Wisconsin

Food: earthworms from plowed fields, fish, insects, carrion (remains of dead animals), garbage and rodents

Nesting: May to June

Nest: 12" saucer-shaped ground nest made of weeds, grasses and debris on islands or lakeshores; nest in large colonies

Eggs: average clutch 3; light brown with brown, lavender and gray markings; 1 brood per year

Young: hatch covered with downy feathers in about 21 days; fully mature at 3 years

Predators: birds including great horned owls, peregrine falcon and larger gulls at nest colonies; foxes, weasels, raccoons and domestic cats

Migration: most migrate to southern states and Mexico; some spend the winter along Lake Michigan

Description: The Ring-billed Gull is named for the dark ring around the tip of its yellow bill. The legs and feet are greenish yellow. Its body is white with gray wings that have white-spotted, black tips. The tail is white with a dark band at the tip.

birds

soaring

DID YOU KNOW...? The Red-tail is a powerful raptor (bird of prey). Its eyesight is many times greater than a human's, and it can see a small mouse or rat from hundreds of feet in the air. Listen for its high-pitched screams. Watch as it circles above its prey, then dives down to snatch it with its sharp talons. The hawk has a sharp, curved beak adapted for tearing its prey into pieces as it eats. The Red-tailed Hawk is often seen perched on trees and telephone poles along highways.

HAWK, RED-TAILED
Buteo jamaicensis

Size: body 19–26" long; 4–4½' wingspan; males 1½–2 lbs.; females 2–4 lbs.

Habitat: swamps, woodlands and prairies

Range: throughout Wisconsin

Food: mice, rabbits, snakes, birds and insects; regurgitates pellets of indigestible parts of prey

Nesting: March to May

Nest: 28–38" across; lined with shredded bark and pine needles; hawk returns to same nest site each year

Eggs: average clutch 2–3; bluish and speckled; 1 brood per year

Young: hatch covered with white down in 28–32 days; leave the nest at 6–7 weeks; both parents tend young

Predators: great horned owls

Migration: migrates to southern states; some remain year-round in southern Wisconsin

Description: The Red-tailed Hawk varies in color from buff to brown to black-and-white, with a patterned, streaked underside. Adults usually have a bright reddish tail.

birds

DID YOU KNOW...? The Great Blue Heron is the largest and most common heron species. Often miscalled a crane, the Great Blue Heron is often spotted hunting along the water's edge. The heron's large 4-toed feet help distribute its weight in the same manner as snowshoes, preventing it from sinking into the mud. It can stand very still as it watches for food.

HERON, GREAT BLUE
Ardea herodias

Size: body 39–52" long; 6–7' wingspan; 6–12 lbs.

Habitat: shallow lakes, ponds, rivers and marshes

Range: throughout Wisconsin

Food: mice, frogs, snails, fish, insects and small birds

Nesting: April to July

Nest: 2–3' across; grouped in large rookeries (colonies) in tall trees along water's edge, nests are built of sticks and often are located more than 100' above the ground; nests are used year after year

Eggs: average clutch 3–6; pale blue-green eggs; 1 brood per year

Young: hatch featherless in 28 days; male and female care for young by regurgitating food into their mouths; young leave nest at 2–4 weeks

Predators: turkey vultures and great horned owls; raccoons prey on eggs and young

Migration: migrates to southern states, Mexico and Central America

Description: The Great Blue Heron has a blue-gray back with lighter undersides. It has a white head with a black crest, long neck, long stick-like dark legs, and a long dagger-like pale yellow bill.

birds

female

male

DID YOU KNOW...? The Ruby-throated Hummingbird flies at speeds of more than 60 mph. It can even fly backwards. Its name comes from the humming sound created by the rapid beating of its tiny wings that move at 50–75 beats per second. It migrates south each winter, flying up to 500 miles without resting. It is attracted to bright flowers and can be seen hovering from flower to flower, feeding on nectar. The Ruby-throated Hummingbird is the only common hummingbird east of the Mississippi River.

HUMMINGBIRD, RUBY-THROATED
Archilochus colubris

Size: body 3¾" long; 4½" wingspan; ⅒ oz. (about the weight of a penny)

Habitat: open wooded areas

Range: throughout Wisconsin

Food: flower nectar, tree sap and spiders

Nesting: May to August

Nest: cup-shaped; about the size of a walnut shell; built from plant material and spider silk; located 10–20' above ground

Eggs: average clutch 2; white; pea-sized; 1–2 broods per year

Young: hatch in 14–16 days; feathers develop at 3–4 days; young leave the nest at 30–34 days

Predators: sharp-shinned hawks and American kestrels

Migration: migrates to southern states, Mexico and Central America

Description: The Ruby-throated Hummingbird is a tiny emerald green bird with light undersides. It has a long, thin bill. Males have a bright red throat patch and females have a white throat patch.

birds

"broken" wing display

DID YOU KNOW...? To protect its nest from predators, the Killdeer performs an elaborate distraction display. Appearing to be injured, it lures predators away from its nest dragging its "broken" wing and plaintively crying. Once the predator has turned its attention away from the nest, the Killdeer quickly flies away.

KILLDEER
Charadrius vociferus

Size: body 8–11" long; 19–24" wingspan; 2½–4½ oz.

Habitat: open areas, plowed fields and beaches

Range: throughout Wisconsin

Food: grasshoppers, beetles, snails and earthworms

Nesting: April–May

Nest: ground nest; shallow, lined depression with no surrounding vegetation

Eggs: average clutch 4; pale buff, heavily spotted; usually 1 brood per year, rarely 2

Young: hatch in 24–26 days, covered in yellow down and able to move and feed themselves; female continues to brood young for several weeks; able to fly at 25 days

Predators: coyotes, foxes, cats; owls, snakes, oppossums, gulls and raccoons prey on eggs and young

Migration: migrates to southern states, Mexico and Central America; usually the first shorebird to arrive each spring and the last to depart

Description: A very familiar plover, the Killdeer is a medium-sized shorebird with a brown back, cap and wings. It has an orange rump, white undersides and two black breast bands. It has long legs, large eyes and a short, thick bill.

birds

DID YOU KNOW...? The bones of most birds are hollow and lightweight, which aids them in flight. In contrast, the loon has solid bones, which helps it to dive to depths up to 150' in search of food. The adults often carry the young on their backs during the first few weeks. A loon's legs are located so far back on its body that it has great difficulty walking on land. It occupies a range of 10–200 acres and spends most of its time in the water searching for food.

LOON, COMMON
Gavia immer

Size: body 28–36" long; 49–58" wingspan; 8–12 lbs.

Habitat: large, deep, clear lakes, usually with islands and bays

Range: northern Wisconsin

Food: fish, crayfish and insects

Nesting: May and June

Nest: 2' across; commonly found on protected shoreline or island

Eggs: average clutch of 2; olive green speckled with brown; 1 brood per year

Young: hatch covered with dark, fuzzy down in 29 days; independent at 2–3 months; both parents care for eggs and young

Predators: bald eagles

Migration: migrates to southern states, Mexico

Description: The Common Loon has a black-and-white checkered back, a dark greenish black head, a long, pointed black bill and bright red eyes.

birds

DID YOU KNOW...? The Barred Owl's right ear is higher than its left ear. This helps the owl to pinpoint the location of its prey by sound alone, though it can also rely on its keen sight. Its sight is 100 times better than a person's. The Barred Owl has a distinctive eight-hoot call that sounds like it's saying "Who cooks for you? Who cooks for all?" The Barred Owl is a favorite prey of the Great Horned Owl.

OWL, BARRED
Strix varia

Size: body 17–24" long; 3½–4' wingspan; 12–23 oz.

Habitat: mature forests, dense wooded areas and swamps

Range: throughout Wisconsin

Food: mice, squirrels, rabbits, birds, frogs, fish and crayfish; regurgitates pellets containing the indigestible parts of its prey, including bones, feathers and hair

Nesting: March to May

Nest: uses tree hollows, abandoned nests of other animals and nest boxes

Eggs: average clutch 2–4; white; 1 brood per year

Young: hatch blind and covered with fine white down in 28–33 days; eyes open at 1 week; flight feathers develop at 6–9 weeks; leave nest at 12–16 weeks

Predators: great horned owls and hawks; weasels and raccoons prey on eggs and young

Migration: present year-round

Description: The Barred Owl is grayish brown with dark rings around its eyes and face. It has a white and brown barred collar, and brown streaked undersides. Its large eyes are dark brown. The female is slightly larger than the male.

birds

female

male

DID YOU KNOW...? The Ring-necked Pheasant will often run for cover rather than fly to avoid danger. However, it is capable of flight speeds of 45 mph for short distances. The average lifespan of a pheasant is less than one year. A non-native species successfully introduced to Wisconsin in 1916, the pheasant is often seen along roadsides ingesting small pebbles, known as grit, which help to break down its food for digestion.

PHEASANT, RING-NECKED
Phasianus colchicus

Size: body 22–35" long including tail; 28–30" wingspan; 2–2¾ lbs.

Habitat: prairies and farmland; cattail marshes for winter cover

Range: southern two-thirds of Wisconsin

Food: grass and weed seeds, crops and insects

Nesting: late March to early May

Nest: hens build nests on the ground, often in hay fields

Eggs: average clutch 12; greenish brown; 1 brood per year

Young: hatch covered with feathers and able to feed themselves in 23–25 days; young are able to fly short distances at 1 week, but they remain with the female for 10–12 weeks

Predators: foxes, coyotes, great horned owls, northern goshawks; raccoons and skunks take eggs

Migration: present year-round

Description: Male Ring-necked Pheasants are coppery brown with black flecks. They have a greenish black head with a red eye patch and a white ring around the neck. Their long tapered tails may reach 15". Females are pale speckled brown with shorter tails.

birds

DID YOU KNOW...? Wisconsin's state bird! An early arrival each spring, the American Robin is usually found poking around lawns in search of earthworms. It occasionally uses anting to rid itself of lice and other parasites. The bird positions itself near an anthill and allows ants to crawl all over its body. A robin is not listening for worms when it cocks its head from side to side. Because its eyes are placed far back on the sides of its head, it must turn its head from side to side to look at things. Robins often form large migrating flocks in the fall.

ROBIN, AMERICAN
Turdus migratorius

Size: body 9–11" long; 17" wingspan; 2–3 oz.

Habitat: open wooded areas, farmland, backyards

Range: throughout Wisconsin

Food: earthworms, insects, fruits and berries

Nesting: early spring

Nest: females build nests out of mud, grass and twigs; found in trees, shrubs and artificial structures

Eggs: average clutch 3–5; pale blue; 2 broods per year

Young: hatch blind and featherless in 12–14 days; eyes open at 1 week; flight feathers develop at 13–20 days

Predators: sharp-shinned hawks, Cooper's hawks, domestic cats; raccoons raid nests

Migration: migrates to southern states and northern Mexico; a few remain year-round in Wisconsin

Description: Male American Robins have slate gray backs, rusty red chests and white speckled throats. Females are brownish gray with pale orange chests.

birds

DID YOU KNOW...? The Barn Swallow feeds while flying. It skims over ponds and fields to catch insects in its wide mouth. It will even take a drink or bathe while flying. The Barn Swallow's nest takes almost 1,000 beakfuls of mud to construct. Each fall it migrates south to areas where insects are plentiful.

SWALLOW, BARN
Hirundo rustica

Size: body 5½–7" long; 11–13" wingspan; about ¾ oz.

Habitat: farmland and open woodlands, often near water

Range: throughout Wisconsin

Food: airborne insects

Nesting: May to August

Nest: small, cup-like nests, made almost entirely of mud and lined with feathers; often located in small colonies on bridges, barns and sheds

Eggs: average clutch 4–5; white with reddish brown spots; 2 broods per year

Young: hatch blind and featherless in 13–17 days; eyes open at 1 week; flight feathers develop at 13–20 days; leave nest at 18–23 days; both parents tend young

Predators: merlins, sharp-shinned hawks

Migration: migrates to South America

Description: The Barn Swallow is dark steel blue with rusty orange undersides. It has a deeply forked tail with white markings.

birds

DID YOU KNOW...? The Tundra Swan is the most common swan species in North America. It is also called the whistling swan due to the whistling-like sound its powerful wings make during flight. It is usually found in flocks of approximately 20–100 birds or more. The male is called a cob. The female is called a pen. The young are called cygnets.

SWAN, TUNDRA
Cygnus columbianus

Size: body 3–5' long; 6½–7' wingspan; 14 lbs.

Habitat: marshes, rivers, lakes, ponds and open fields

Range: throughout Wisconsin

Food: aquatic plants, roots, tubers and seeds; waste crops and unharvested grain; young consume large quantities of invertebrates (e.g., clams)

Nesting: June to July; pairs mate for life

Nest: 12–18"-high mound, usually close to water; nest is used year after year

Eggs: average clutch 2–7 eggs; cream colored; 1 brood per year

Young: hatch in 35–40 days; male and females take turns incubating; fledge in 60–70 days

Predators: eggs and cygnets are taken by foxes, gulls, ravens and weasels

Migration: present in Wisconsin during migration only; nests on the tundra in northern Canada and Alaska; winters on the east coast, including Virginia and North Carolina

Description: The Tundra Swan is smallest swan species in North America. It is all white, with black legs, feet, bill and face. It has a yellow spot located near each eye. The male and female look alike. Immature swans are grayish brown with pinkish bills.

birds

DID YOU KNOW...? The abundant Blue-winged Teal is one of the most widespread ducks in North America. It nests as far north as Alaska. It is a dabbling duck (also called a puddle duck) and feeds with its tail straight up in the air or by skimming the water just below the surface. Like all ducks, the Blue-winged Teal has a lamellate bill, which means it has tooth-like edges on the bill that act like a strainer, allowing the duck to hold a piece of food while the water drains out.

TEAL, BLUE-WINGED
Anas discors

Size: body 15–16" long; 22–24" wingspan; 13–19 oz.

Habitat: shallow lakes and ponds, prairie potholes and marshes

Range: throughout Wisconsin

Food: aquatic plants, seeds, insects and invertebrates (e.g., snails and clams)

Nesting: May and June

Nest: ground nest in heavy vegetation; female constructs the nest

Eggs: average clutch 6–15; cream colored; 1 brood per year

Young: hatch in 23–27 days; fledge in 35–44 days

Predators: foxes, skunks, raccoons and coyotes prey on eggs; turtles, large fish and domestic cats prey on nestlings

Migration: migrates to southern states, Mexico, Central America and northern South America

Description: The Blue-winged Teal is a small duck with a dark bill. Its plumage is brownish gray, speckled with black. It has a light, powder blue wing patch located on the front portion of each wing, which is usually only visible when it is flying. Males have a white crescent on the face and a white patch on the tail in spring.

birds

DID YOU KNOW...? Wild Turkeys commonly form flocks of six or more birds and roost in trees each evening. In spring, males perform elaborate courtship displays to attract females. In 1782, it lost by a single vote to the Bald Eagle as the national bird. In 1900 the Wild Turkey population was less than 100,000 due to habitat loss. It was extirpated from Wisconsin in the 1890s, but was successfully reintroduced in the mid-1970s. Today, thanks to better wildlife management, Wild Turkey numbers have grown to nearly 7 million nationwide.

TURKEY, WILD
Meleagris gallopavo

Size: body 3–4' long; 5' wingspan; males weigh 16–25 lbs.; females weigh 9–11 lbs.

Habitat: open wooded areas and brushy grasslands

Range: west central and southern Wisconsin

Food: ferns, grass, buds, berries, insects and acorns

Nesting: April to June

Nest: hens build nest on the ground, usually a leaf-lined hollow in heavy brush

Eggs: average clutch 10–18; buff with tan markings; 1 brood per year

Young: hatch covered with feathers and able to feed themselves in 28 days; young are able to fly at 3–4 weeks, but remain with the female for up to 4 months; young are called poults

Predators: coyote, great horned owls

Migration: present year-round

Description: The Wild Turkey is a large dark brown and black bird with a fan tail. Males (called toms) have wattles (fleshy growths that hang beneath the chin), spurs (bony spear-like projections on the back of each leg), a snood (a flap of skin that drapes over the bill), and a hair-like chest beard. Females (called hens) are more drab. They are strong short-distance flyers but prefer to walk.

DID YOU KNOW...? The American Woodcock is also known as the timberdoodle and the bog sucker. It has large eyes and nearly full circle vision. Its long bill has highly sensitive nerve endings that can detect the movement of earthworms beneath the soil. In spite of its short wings, the American Woodcock is capable of flight speeds of 30 mph. In spring, the male makes flight displays at sunset while creating a twittering sound with his wings to court females.

WOODCOCK, AMERICAN
Scolopax minor

Size: body 10–12" long; 18" wingspan; 8–10 oz.

Habitat: open wooded areas and wetlands

Range: throughout Wisconsin

Food: earthworms, grubs and insects

Nesting: April to June

Nest: ground nest; measures 4–5" across

Eggs: average clutch 4; buff-colored with brown specks; 1 brood per year

Young: hatch covered with down and able to feed themselves in 20–21 days; reach adult size at 25 days and are able to fly; fully independent at 6–8 weeks

Predators: foxes and coyotes; raccoons may take eggs

Migration: migrates to southern states

Description: The reclusive American Woodcock is a cinnamon-colored bird with dark brown splotches and extensive barring. Its pinkish legs, neck, tail and wings are short. It is most active at night and early in the morning; look for rectangular holes (⅛" wide) in the soil made by its probing bill.

birds

female

male

DID YOU KNOW...? The Pileated Woodpecker is the largest woodpecker in Wisconsin. With its strong neck muscles, a thick skull, and short feathers that keep sawdust out of its nostrils, it is highly adapted to drilling holes in trees. Instead of being attached to the bottom of its mouth, the woodpecker's tongue is attached between its nostrils and reaches around the back of the skull and into the mouth. Specialized muscles work to contract and extend its tongue.

WOODPECKER, PILEATED
Dryocopus pileatus

Size: body 16–19½" long; 27–30" wingspan; 10–16 oz.

Habitat: wooded areas

Range: west central and northern Wisconsin

Food: berries, fruits, nuts, insects and insect larvae

Nesting: April to May; pairs mate for life

Nest: male and female begin construction of a nesting cavity in February; rectangular or oval in shape with an 8" opening; usually located 40' above the forest floor on the south side of a tree

Eggs: average clutch 4; white; 1 brood per year

Young: hatch blind and featherless in 18 days; eyes open at 1 week; flight feathers develop at 13–20 days; independent at 6 months; both parents tend young

Predators: hawks and owls; gray foxes, weasels and squirrels prey on eggs and young

Migration: present year-round

Description: The Pileated Woodpecker is Wisconsin's largest woodpecker. It has a black back, and a white neck and throat. It has a red crest, black chisel-like bill and a long spear-like tongue. Males have a red mustache.

LIFELIST

Place a check by each mammal or bird you've seen whether in your backyard, on a camping trip or at the zoo

Critters

☐ Badger, American

    Location: _____ Date: _____

    Comments: _____

☐ Bat, Little Brown

    Location: _____ Date: _____

    Comments: _____

☐ Bear, Black

    Location: _____ Date: _____

    Comments: _____

☐ Beaver, American

    Location: _____ Date: _____

    Comments: _____

☐ Bobcat

    Location: _____ Date: _____

    Comments: _____

☐ Chipmunk, Eastern

    Location: _____ Date: _____

    Comments: _____

☐ Cottontail, Eastern

    Location: _____ Date: _____

    Comments: _____

☐ Coyote

Location: _____ Date: _____

Comments: _____

☐ Deer, White-tailed

Location: _____ Date: _____

Comments: _____

☐ Elk

Location: _____ Date: _____

Comments: _____

☐ Fox, Red

Location: _____ Date: _____

Comments: _____

☐ Hare, Snowshoe

Location: _____ Date: _____

Comments: _____

☐ Mink

Location: _____ Date: _____

Comments: _____

☐ Muskrat

Location: _____ Date: _____

Comments: _____

☐ Opossum, Virginia

Location: _____ Date: _____

Comments: _____

☐ Otter, Northern River

Location: _____ Date: _____

Comments: _____

☐ Porcupine, North American
Location: _____ Date: _____
Comments: _____

☐ Raccoon, Northern
Location: _____ Date: _____
Comments: _____

☐ Skunk, Striped
Location: _____ Date: _____
Comments: _____

☐ Squirrel, Eastern Fox
Location: _____ Date: _____
Comments: _____

☐ Squirrel, Thirteen-lined Ground
Location: _____ Date: _____
Comments: _____

☐ Vole, Meadow
Location: _____ Date: _____
Comments: _____

☐ Weasel, Long-tailed
Location: _____ Date: _____
Comments: _____

☐ Wolf, Gray
Location: _____ Date: _____
Comments: _____

☐ Woodchuck
Location: _____ Date: _____
Comments: _____

Birds

☐ Blackbird, Red-winged

  Location: _____ Date: _____

  Comments: _____

☐ Bluebird, Eastern

  Location: _____ Date: _____

  Comments: _____

☐ Cardinal, Northern

  Location: _____ Date: _____

  Comments: _____

☐ Chickadee, Black-capped

  Location: _____ Date: _____

  Comments: _____

☐ Crane, Sandhill

  Location: _____ Date: _____

  Comments: _____

☐ Crane, Whooping

  Location: _____ Date: _____

  Comments: _____

☐ Eagle, Bald

  Location: _____ Date: _____

  Comments: _____

☐ Goose, Canada

  Location: _____ Date: _____

  Comments: _____

☐ Grouse, Ruffed

  Location: _____ Date: _____

  Comments: _____

☐ Gull, Ring-billed

Location: _____ Date: _____

Comments: _____

☐ Hawk, Red-tailed

Location: _____ Date: _____

Comments: _____

☐ Heron, Great Blue

Location: _____ Date: _____

Comments: _____

☐ Hummingbird, Ruby-throated

Location: _____ Date: _____

Comments: _____

☐ Killdeer

Location: _____ Date: _____

Comments: _____

☐ Loon, Common

Location: _____ Date: _____

Comments: _____

☐ Owl, Barred

Location: _____ Date: _____

Comments: _____

☐ Pheasant, Ring-necked

Location: _____ Date: _____

Comments: _____

☐ Robin, American

Location: _____ Date: _____

Comments: _____

☐ Swallow, Barn

Location: _____ Date: _____

Comments: _____

☐ Swan, Tundra

Location: _____ Date: _____

Comments: _____

☐ Teal, Blue-winged

Location: _____ Date: _____

Comments: _____

☐ Turkey, Wild

Location: _____ Date: _____

Comments: _____

☐ Woodcock, American

Location: _____ Date: _____

Comments: _____

☐ Woodpecker, Pileated

Location: _____ Date: _____

Comments: _____

WILD WORDS

A

Adaptation: a particular characteristic developed by a plant or animal that makes it better suited to its environment.

Altricial: baby birds that are helpless and naked when hatched. Altricial chicks require a great deal of care from their parents.

Amphibians: cold-blooded, smooth-skinned vertebrates that spend part of their life on land and part of their life in the water including frogs, toads, newts and salamanders.

Anthropomorphism: attributing human characteristics to animals.

Antler: bony projections grown and shed each year by members of the deer family, typically males. Antlers are used in courtship rivalries between competing males.

B

Behavior: the way in which an animal responds to its environment.

Brood: (noun) the offspring of birds hatched at one time; (verb) to hatch, protect and warm the young, usually done instinctively by the female.

Browse: (noun) portions of woody plants including twigs, shoots and leaves used as food by animals such as deer; (verb) to eat parts of woody plants.

Brumation: a period of winter dormancy brought on by dropping temperatures during which a reptile's or amphibian's body processes are slowed down, and they become immobile.

Buck: a male deer, goat, pronghorn or rabbit.

Bull: a male moose, elk or bison.

Burrow: (noun) a hole, tunnel or underground den excavated by an animal for shelter or refuge; (verb) to dig underground.

camouflage: a protective adaptation that enables an animal to disguise itself or blend with its surroundings.

carnivore: an animal that eats other animals; a meat eater.

carrion: the body of a dead animal in the natural state of decay, which serves as a food source for other animals.

clutch: a nest of eggs.

cold-blooded (ectothermic): an animal whose body temperature is dependent upon and varies with the temperature of its environment (e.g., fish, amphibians and reptiles).

communication: sound, scent or behavior recognized by members of the same species and sometimes by other species.

competition: different species of animals that use the same source for food or shelter.

conservation: the care, wise use and management of a resource.

consumer: an animal that gets its food from producers (plants).

courtship: a behavior or series of actions an animal displays to indicate to the opposite sex that it is ready to mate in order to reproduce.

cover: naturally occurring sheltered areas that provide concealment and shelter for wildlife, such as a dead tree, fallen log, rock outcrops, dense areas of brush or trees.

cow: a female moose, wapiti (elk) or bison.

crepuscular: active in twilight at dawn and dusk.

diurnal: active during the day.

Doe: a female deer, pronghorn or rabbit.

Down: a layer of soft, fine feathers that provides insulation.

Drake: a male duck.

E

Ecology: the study of the relationships between living things and the environments in which they live.

Ecosystem: an interacting system of plants, animals, soil and climactic conditions in a self-contained environment (e.g., pond, marsh, swamp, lake or stream).

Endangered: a species in danger of becoming extinct due to declining population numbers.

Environment: the entire surroundings of an organism (plant or animal) or group of organisms.

Estuary: area where fresh water and salt water meet.

Ethics: principles of good conduct; a sense of right and wrong.

Exotic: a foreign species introduced to an area from another region or ecosystem. Exotic species are considered undesirable as they compete with native species for habitat and food.

Extinct: a species that no longer exists or has died out.

F

Fledgling: young birds learning to fly.

Food chain: plants and animals linked together as sources and consumers of food; typically an organism higher in the food chain eats one lower in the food chain, so the health of one is dependent on the health of another.

Food web: the many possible feeding relationships found within a given ecosystem.

orage: (noun) plant material such as grasses, ferns, shrubs and the leaves and twigs of trees; (verb) to eat plant material.

G

ame species: wildlife that can be hunted or trapped according to legal seasons and limits.

estation: length of pregnancy.

H

abitat: the local environment in which an animal lives. Components include food, water, cover (shelter) and space.

abitat enhancement: the development and improvement of habitat (including sources of food, water, cover and space) for the benefit of fish or wildlife.

en: a female pheasant, duck, quail or turkey.

erbivore: an animal that eats only plant material.

ibernation: a period of winter dormancy during which an animal's body processes slow dramatically, reducing the amount of energy required for survival. True hibernators' body processes slow nearly to a stop, and they require much less energy to survive. Deep sleepers' body processes do not slow as much, and they are more easily awakened.

ome range: the area over which an animal repeatedly travels in order to locate food, water and cover.

orn: hard protrusions that continuously grow on the head of certain mammals such as the bighorn sheep and bison. Horns are made of keratin, the same material that makes fingernails.

ncubate: to warm eggs (usually bird eggs) with body heat so they develop and hatch. Females typically incubate the eggs.

Introduced species: a plant or animal brought from another region often another continent, either intentionally or by accident; introduced species can have positive or negative effects on the native species. Also referred to as "exotic" or "non-native," especially when the result is negative.

Invertebrates: animals without backbones, including insects earthworms, spiders and mollusks (e.g. snails).

J-L

Land ethic: deliberate, thoughtful and responsible consideration for the natural landscape and natural resources, including wildlife fossil fuels, soil, water and timber.

Land management: the purposeful manipulation of land or habitat by people to encourage wildlife populations to increase decrease or stabilize in number. In the case of wildlife, this involves managing food, water, cover and space to affect population numbers.

Larva: the newly hatched, earliest stage that differs greatly from the appearance and form of the adult; usually used in relation to insects, but sometimes also for amphibians.

M

Mammal: a warm-blooded animal that has fur or hair and produces milk to feed its young.

Migration: the seasonal movements of fish and wildlife from one area to another usually triggered by length of daylight hours Animals that move varying distances at irregular times dependent upon weather and availability of food are partial migrators Animals that move to the same places at the same times every year are complete migrators.

N

Native: an indigenous or naturally occurring species of plant or animal.

Natural resource: materials found in nature to which people have assigned value such as timber, fresh water, wildlife and fossil fuels (coal and oil).

Nocturnal: an animal that is active by night.

Nongame species: the majority of wildlife not hunted by humans including songbirds, raptors, reptiles and amphibians.

Nonrenewable resources: nonliving natural resources which, for all practical purposes, cannot be replaced, including metallic minerals (e.g. gold and copper) and fossil fuels (e.g. coal and oil).

O

Omnivore: an animal that eats both plants and animals (meat).

Opportunist: an animal that can take advantage of any number of food sources available.

P

Pheromone: a chemical scent secreted as a means of communication between members of the same species.

Photosynthesis: the process by which plant cells convert light, water and carbon dioxide into energy and nutrients while simultaneously releasing oxygen.

Plumage: the feathers of a bird.

Pollution: toxic (poisonous) substances deposited in the air, water or soil creating an unhealthy environment.

Population: a collection of individuals of the same species in a given area whose members can breed with one another.

Precocial: baby birds that hatch covered in down and able to move about on their own.

Predator: an animal that hunts and feeds on other animals (prey).

Prey: an animal hunted or killed for food by other animals (predators).

Producers: plants that obtain energy from the sun and produce food through the process of photosynthesis.

Q-R

Range: the particular geographic region in which a species is found.

Raptor: a bird of prey; includes falcons, owls, eagles, hawks, kites, vultures and ospreys.

Recreation: an activity undertaken for enjoyment; entertainment, often associated with natural resources (water, forests, rock formations) includes rock climbing, bird watching, fishing, canoeing and hunting.

Renewable natural resource: a natural resource that can be replenished and harvested, including trees and wildlife.

Reptiles: cold-blooded vertebrate animals that have scales or hard plates covering their bodies (e.g., snakes, lizards and turtles).

Riparian area: lands adjacent to streams, rivers, lakes and other wetlands where the vegetation is influenced by the great availability of water.

Roost: refers to a safe gathering place used by wildlife, usually birds and bats, for rest or sleep.

Rut: activity associated with breeding behavior of deer family (e.g., white-tailed deer, moose, elk).

S

Scat: refers to defecation, excrement or waste.

Scavenger: an animal that feeds on the remains of dead animals.

Scrape: an area where concentrated amounts of urine are mixed with mud to attract a mate or indicate territory.

Season: time of year when game species may be legally harvested.

Sow: a female bear.

Species: a group of animals that have similar structure, common ancestors and characteristics they maintain through breeding.

Stewardship: responsible care of natural resources for future generations.

Stocking: the artificial propagation and introduction of game species into an area.

Territory: the area an animal will defend, usually during breeding season, against intruders of its own species.

Threatened: a classification for wildlife species whose population is in great decline and approaching the "endangered" classification.

U-V

Vertebrates: animals with a backbone, including fish, birds, mammals, reptiles and amphibians.

W-Z

Warm-blooded (endothermic): an animal whose body temperature is unrelated to its environment (e.g., mammals and birds).

Wean: to withhold mother's milk from young and substitute other nourishment.

Wildlife: nondomesticated plants and animals (including mammals, birds, fish, reptiles, insects and amphibians).

Wildlife agency: a state or federal organization responsible for managing wildlife.

Wildlife management: a combination of techniques, scientific knowledge and technical skills used to protect, conserve and manage wildlife and habitat.

Winter kill: the death of animals during winter resulting from lack of food and exposure to cold.

WILDLIFE FOREVER PROJECTS IN WISCONSIN

Working at the grassroots level, Wildlife Forever (WF) ha partnered on successful conservation projects in all 50 states

- Reintroduced an elk herd in Chequamegon-Nicolet Nationa Forest near Clam Lake.

- Researched black bear population dynamics on Stockton Islan in Lake Superior.

- Conserved stream habitat and fish passage by removing dam on the Deerskin and Milwaukee Rivers.

- Protected water quality on Silver Lake and wildlife habita through restoration of the surrounding watershed.

- Conserved over 200 wetland basins throughout Wisconsin.

- Restored 1,000 feet of shoreline on the Oconto River.

- Conducted public education and outreach by implementin Watchable Wildlife interpretive programs.

- Restored nesting sites for the endangered Forster's tern.

- Studied water quality and trout habitat on the Kinnickinnic Rive

- Conserved fisheries statewide by stocking fingerlings and fr installing aerators in lakes and ponds, maintaining hatchery an nursery facilities, and restoring lakeshores and stream banks.

RULER

Find tracks? Use this guide to measure them.

inches

centimeters

0 1 2 3 4 5 6 7 8 9